Ketogenic Bread:

Quick Guide for Starting Low Carb Keto Bread Diet. For Absolute Beginners. Short Reads.

Table of Contents

Introduction......5
Chapter 1: What is Ketogenic Bread......7

Keto Bread Tips

> *Eggs*
> *Butter and Oil*
> *All the Dry Ingredients*
> *Additional Tips*

Chapter 2: Benefits of Ketogenic Bread......14

Additional Keto Bread Benefits

> *Almond Flour*
> *Eggs*
> *Coconut Oil*

Chapter 3: What You Can Achieve With Ketogenic Bread......20

General Achievements
Specific Achievements

Chapter 4: How to Start the Ketogenic Diet with Ketogenic Bread......29

Starting the Keto Diet

Chapter 5: Anti-aging, Weight Loss, and More......35

Weight Loss
Anti-aging
Chronic Inflammation Management

Conclusion......41

© Copyright 2019 by Chantel Stephens - All rights reserved.

This content is provided with the sole purpose of providing relevant information on a specific topic for which every reasonable effort has been made to ensure that it is both accurate and reasonable. Nevertheless, by purchasing this content you consent to the fact that the author, as well as the publisher, are in no way experts on the topics contained herein, regardless of any claims as such that may be made within. As such, any suggestions or recommendations that are made within are done so purely for entertainment value. It is recommended that you always consult a professional prior to undertaking any of the advice or techniques discussed within.

This is a legally binding declaration that is considered both valid and fair by both the Committee of Publishers Association and the American Bar Association and should be considered as legally binding within the United States.

The reproduction, transmission, and duplication of any of the content found herein, including any specific or extended information will be done as an illegal act regardless of the end form the information ultimately takes. This includes copied versions of the work both physical, digital, and audio unless express consent of the Publisher is provided beforehand. Any additional rights reserved.

Furthermore, the information that can be found within the pages described forthwith shall be considered both accurate and truthful when it comes to the recounting of facts. As such, any use, correct or incorrect, of the provided information will render the Publisher free of responsibility as to the actions taken outside of their direct purview. Regardless, there are zero scenarios where the original author or the Publisher can be deemed liable in any fashion for any damages or hardships that may result from any of the information discussed herein.

Additionally, the information in the following pages is intended only for informational purposes and should thus be thought of as universal. As befitting its nature, it is presented without assurance regarding its prolonged validity or interim quality. Trademarks that are mentioned are done without written consent and can in no way be considered an endorsement from the trademark holder.

Introduction

I want to thank you and congratulate you for downloading *Ketogenic Bread*.

As you begin researching methods for taking control of your life, weight, and health, you can sometimes end up with a lot of information that can be overwhelming. There is a lot of research and information out there. Some of it even contradicting each other convincingly. This is why it is so important for you to recognize how and why you are embarking on a certain path, such as following the Keto diet. One such contradictory review you may encounter on the Keto diet is about Keto bread. The purpose of this book is to reveal the correlation between the Keto diet and Keto bread, as well as the unique benefits of introducing this food into your Keto diet, can provide to you.

The Keto diet is nothing new. It has been used for years as a medical treatment, but it did spend a long time "sitting on the shelf" as newer medical interventions became more popular. But Keto is enjoying a "comeback," and with the addition of the Internet, more people than ever are recognizing and enjoying the benefits of this lifestyle. More and more research continues to be published about this eating plan and how it impacts your health. There is still plenty of room for more research, and there are plenty of precautions you should follow, but overall this diet is a sustainable and healthy approach to eating most anyone can follow.

Another added benefit of the Internet and the resurgence of the keto diet is the increase in healthy, "approved," and delicious recipes for Keto bread. As you start exploring Keto bread more in depth, thank you again for choosing this book. I hope you find it informative and enjoyable!

Chapter 1: What is Ketogenic Bread

The Keto diet, also known as the Ketogenic diet, is an eating plan focused on high fat and low carbohydrates. The purpose of the diet is to help you burn fat cells more efficiently. More than 50 various studies have shown that following this meal plan is helpful for weight loss, performance improvement, and well-being. Because of its health benefits, many doctors recommend this diet to their patients. It has been used to help reverse type-2 diabetes in patients, as well as helping obese patients lose excessive amounts of body weight without feeling the pangs of hunger often.

The word keto is derived from the term ketones, which are the little molecules in your body that are used for energy. They are the "back up" fuel supply for when the body runs out of glucose, or blood sugar, to use for energy. Creating ketones requires eating a diet with minimal carbs and moderate protein. Carbohydrates are processed in your body into glucose, and protein is also sometimes broken down into blood sugar. Instead of relying on food to supply glucose, your liver creates ketones from fat cells. These then fuel your body, especially fueling your brain. Your brain requires a lot of energy to function properly. It cannot be fueled directly from fat, but it can thrive on glucose or ketones.

When you follow this eating strategy you encourage your body to burn fat all day, consistently. As insulin levels drop and stabilize your body increase fat burning significantly. This switch allows your body to tap into the fat stores and begin burning them off. This is why people see dramatic weight loss when starting this diet. The other benefits, which are often less obvious on the outside, include feeling less hungry and having a steady level of energy. These assist you in being focused and alert more often.

Ketosis is the term applied to the state of your body when you are burning fat for energy and not glucose. This metabolic state can occur while fasting, which is also the fastest method for entering ketosis; however, the problem with this method is that you cannot last forever. Following the Keto diet is possible for a long-term diet strategy. It offers a lot of the same benefits of fasting, without actually having to stop eating. Of course, this is not a diet for everyone and it is best to consult your medical professional before embarking on this meal plan. For example, if you are breastfeeding, pregnant, taking medication for diabetes, or on blood pressure medicine you should proceed with caution and medical supervision.

There are still debates and concerns regarding this diet. The purpose of this book is to explain some of the potential benefits of the Keto diet

It may be possible to find a local bakery or grocery store that carries branded, premade Keto bread, but more than likely your best option is to make your own. There are many recipes available to help you make your own, but here are a few tips to help make sure your bread is the best.

Keto Bread Tips

Sometimes Keto bread can taste strongly of eggs, one of the primary ingredients in most recipes. Or it can crumble at your touch. There are some things you can add to your recipe to help avoid this from happening, like adding xanthum gum, to help bind the ingredients together.

Eggs

First and foremost, always allow your eggs to reach room temperature before adding them to the recipe. This is the best way to avoid the egg taste in the bread.

Butter and Oil

Also, allow your butter to reach room temperature, this way the process moves faster for you. Kerrygold butter is a great option for Keto bread. Cut it up, throw the chunks into a frying pan, and let them start melting. Once you see it is melting, remove the pan from the heat and let it continue to melt. This is so your butter is not too hot when you add it to the eggs. Once melted, add your refined coconut oil. Refined is necessary so you do not have the coconut taste.

All the Dry Ingredients

Whisk all the dry ingredients together in a small bowl and then slowly add it to the wet ingredients. Go little by little to make sure it incorporates well.

Additional Tips

- Cook in a glass or silicone bread pan. If glass, drop the oven temperature by 20 degrees.
- When done cooking, remove from the tray and let it cool completely on a bread rack. Again, this helps reduce the taste of eggs.
- If you do not have or want to use xanthum gum, try ground chia seeds, guar gum, or gelatin powder instead.
- You can also use different flours, like coconut and sesame seed.
- Best to store this bread in the fridge or freezer.
- The net carbs for most Keto bread recipes are one!
- For two slices of bread, you can expect about 234 calories. This is higher because of the butter and oil.

consume a glass of wine a day without increasing your net carbs too high!

The foods to avoid on the Keto diet are mainly foods that all people should avoid or limit; refined foods, foods with a lot of sugar, starchy foods, and foods high in carbohydrates. The challenge is that in the Western diet, the most common foods are high-protein, high-carb. In addition, for a long time fat was considered dieting's "enemy." Therefore, a lot of food is stripped of nutritional value in order to strip away the fat. This means many options are considered low-fat. All of this goes directly against the scientific backing of the Keto diet and the meal plans. It also makes it hard for people to switch. Giving up carbohydrates is especially difficult, like cutting out potatoes, rice, noodles, and bread.

One of the best ways to make the switch to Keto "easier" on you is to learn all you can about the Keto bread options. This allows you to still have toast with your eggs in the morning, or pack a sandwich for lunch, or have a piece of bread with your soup for dinner. Having Keto bread on hand helps ease the transition. Eventually, you may find yourself happy to not have bread around, but until then, this is a good Keto "staple" alternative. Keto bread is made from flour-alternative, healthy fats, eggs, and usually xanthum gum. It looks and often tastes like wheat bread, but has on average about 20 times fewer carbohydrates than traditional bread.

and ketogenic bread; however, it is not designed to diagnose or treat medical problems. Make sure to work directly with your medical team to develop a plan that is right for you, including your diet.

Normally you would not find bread listed on an "approved foods" list for the Keto diet. There are several foods that you can enjoy, including many vegetables, fruits, and protein sources. On the other hand, foods high in sugar and carbohydrates, like traditional bread, are usually on the "rejected foods" lists. The mix of food eaten is designed to keep your carbohydrate intake low so that you can enter and remain in ketosis. For most people, this means keeping net carbs below at least 50 grams. If possible, try to get your net carbs under 20 per day. In the beginning, you may find yourself counting carbs a lot, but the more comfortable you get with the "approved" list of foods and understanding how many net carbs are in typical Keto bread, you can eat Keto easily, without spending time counting your carbohydrate intake.

For those following this diet, once you figure out the food, you may need to also look at what you drink. For example, water, coffee, and tea are good beverages to consume; however, not if you are adding flavorings or sugar to them. A controlled and small splash or cream or milk in your tea or coffee is ok, as long as you count the carbs in your daily intake. You can even

Chapter 2: Benefits of Ketogenic Bread

When you begin a diet you need to first understand what is good to eat on the eating plan and what is not. This way you can get the benefits of the diet without unintentionally sabotaging your goals. This advice goes for any diet plan but is especially true for the Keto diet. This is because your body needs to enter into ketosis for you to reap the benefits of eating this way. The only way for your body to get there is by eating a low amount of carbs and limited protein. If you do not eat this way, intentionally or unintentionally, you will not enter into this metabolic state. This means you need to be prepared so you can enjoy the benefits.

As you get started, you may look at the list of foods to avoid and think there is no way that you can cut those out of your diet without sacrifice. You may even be reading this book because you do not think you can give up bread altogether. What you may find, after you enter into ketosis for the first time, is that your cravings disappear. Your body craves the carbohydrates and glucose of those foods, not the foods themselves. This is because the carbs create energy, and your body craves fuel. Once your body begins to fuel itself with its fat stores and rids itself of the excess blood sugar, your cravings subside.

Still, the mental roadblock of letting go of some of your favorite foods, like bread and sweets, can be challenging. This is why there are thousands of different alternatives that you can buy or make to help you ease into the diet plan. Bread is one of the best ways to replace a typically high-carb food with an alternative.

After all, bread is a big deal in most societies. Most people eat bread in some form every day. It is an easy addition to a meal or can be the center of a meal as well. Sandwiches are a simple, on-the-go option, and are easy to find everywhere. This is probably the primary reason why many people look at the Keto diet plan and turn the other way. They do not think they can give up bread completely.

The challenge with traditional bread is the trouble grains cause in your system. If you are not allergic to gluten, chances are that you are sensitive to it to some degree. This is because the human body is not designed to handle large amounts of this ingredient in our diets. It is hard to process and use as fuel, so your body tries to figure it out, creating a host of reactions and responses that are not "normal." As you cut away grains, you will also cut away a lot of carbs. This then leads to cutting away glucose, kicking your body into ketosis, allowing it to burn fat instead of blood sugar for energy.

Here is a basic list of foods you want to cut out on your Keto diet or find alternatives, like Keto bread instead of regular bread:

1. Pasta
2. Rice
3. Oats
4. Flour
5. Potatoes
6. Bread

You can adapt recipes and options for making Keto bread to fit into your daily life. One of the best benefits for eating Keto bread is that it is easy to substitute for your daily foods, but also helps you in reducing your carb intake so you skip into ketosis faster, without feeling like you gave up your normal eating habits. Eventually, then your body no longer craves the large carb load it is used to, you will no longer crave traditional bread. You may find that you no longer want bread at all, or you will prefer the process and taste of your Keto bread to traditional alternatives.

Making the adjustment to low-carb can be surprisingly tricky. And it can be especially challenging if you have a sweet tooth. For example, almost all sodas and desserts are off the menu on a Keto diet. Things like ice cream and pastries are not approved. But a lot of fruit can get on the "bad" list, too. Fruit juice especially is something you will want to avoid. A small serving of berries, like blueberries or raspberries, are good, but in moderation. You may think it is hard at first giving up these sweet treats, but you can substitute them for things like Keto "fat bombs." But like bread, your cravings may dissipate with time as your body gets used to functioning without them. A nice alternative to a sweet treat is to make a sweet bread. This can be done in the cooking process by adding different things to the recipe, or you can do a "French bread" style Keto toast and top with a handful of fresh berries and a sprinkle of cinnamon.

Another one to look out for is a lot of vegetables. It is surprising how many common vegetables have a large number of carbohydrates. This is a sneaky ingredient that can knock you out of ketosis if you are not watching out. This is another reason why it is important to be aware of what is "approved" for the Keto diet, and what is not. This way you can stay on track easier.

Additional Keto Bread Benefits

The ingredients in most Keto bread is what makes it amazing for you. Here is a breakdown of the common ingredients and what they can do for you and your diet:

Almond Flour

The primary ingredient in bread, as well as Keto bread, is flour. In most recipes, you will find almond flour for a variety of reasons. To make this flour you can blanch plain almonds and grind them into a fine powder or purchase it premade from the store. It is rich in antioxidants, vitamin E, and magnesium. It is very low in carbs, but also high in fiber and healthy fat, an ideal combo for the Keto diet. Finally, it is also shown to help lower LDL cholesterol, or the "bad" cholesterol, making it better for your heart.

Eggs

Another common ingredient in Keto bread is an egg. This protein-packed, an inexpensive ingredient is rich in B vitamins, especially B2. The whites are especially high in protein, but the whites do not have the fat like the yolks do. In addition to the B2, eggs are rich in vitamin D, B6, B12, selenium, zinc, copper, and iron. An additional benefit to eggs is the nine amino acids necessary for you to absorb for a healthy diet. There are not many "complete" proteins that off all those amino acids in one serving. Several of the nutrients in eggs, like choline and betaine, are heart-healthy, helping reduce the risk of heart disease and stroke.

Coconut Oil

This "super food" is and another common ingredient found in Keto bread. It is rich in fatty acids and healthy fats. It is ideal for helping your body create more ketones for energy. In addition to creating a clean energy source, it also helps in burning other fats stored in your body. Obesity plagues a vast majority of the world's population, meaning these people have an excess of fat stored in their body. Coconut oil helps burn this fat for energy, especially when in ketosis.

Chapter 3: What You Can Achieve With Ketogenic Bread

There are many things you can expect to benefit from when following the Keto diet and making and eating Keto bread. In this chapter, there are two lists for you—one to describe the general things you can expect to achieve, and the second lists more specific benefits related to Keto bread and bread alternatives.

General Achievements

The first and foremost benefit of the Keto diet is weight loss. Fueling your body with fat takes more energy than using glucose. This means you will burn through your fat at a much higher rate than on any other diet plan. In addition, this diet plan is superior to many others because you do not need to be hungry.

Another achievement you can expect to enjoy is clearer skin. Acne and other skin problems are the results of various causes. Some of those major causes occur through diet and glucose. Refined and processed carbs are known to wreak havoc on skin. These foods mess with the bacteria in your gut. This alteration causes fluctuations in your blood sugar. Both of these can alter your skin. This means that lowering your carb intake can also help you clear up skin problems, like stubborn acne or eczema.

Perhaps one of the most important achievements you can benefit from is the reduced risk of cancer. There have been several studies conducted related to the Keto diet and how it can help prevent and even treat various forms of cancer. In one study Keto was reviewed as a suitable companion to cancer treatment, such as radiation and chemotherapy. This is because cancer cells react more to oxidative stress than normal ones. Complications from high blood sugar and insulin resistance can also lead to an increased risk for certain cancers, which means lowering and stabilizing blood sugar and insulin response can help lower these risks.

In addition to helping prevent and treat cancer, following a Keto diet can also help lower cardiac disease, which is a health concern many Americans face. This is primarily credited to lower cholesterol, a major benefit to following the Keto diet. LDL, or the "bad" cholesterol, drops significantly, while HDL or the "good" cholesterol increases. This only comes about when you follow the diet properly and in a healthy manner, which includes eating healthy foods, like Keto bread.

Your brain may also be positively impacted. There is more research needed in this area; however, many results do suggest that there are benefits to the Keto diet and protecting your brain. It is likely that it can protect against diseases like Alzheimer's and Parkinson's, as well as help treat other issues, like sleeping trouble. One study, in particular, found that children who followed a Keto diet exhibited better cognitive functioning as well as more alertness. Another study found that children with epilepsy also benefited from the Keto diet. Ketosis is shown to help reduce seizures. But more definitive research is needed to prove this connection between the Keto diet and the brain.

Finally, another achievement you can expect is especially for women suffering from PCOS, or polycystic ovarian syndrome. This is a disorder in the endocrine system that results in enlarged ovaries and creation of cysts. If a woman suffers from this disease eating a diet high in carbs can aggravate it. There are not many studies concluded on this topic; however, one pilot study did show women were able to balance their hormones, improved fasting insulin, and stabilize the luteinizing hormone and follicle-stimulating hormone ratios.

Of course, this does not come without risk. Especially, if you are first beginning this new diet plan, you could experience things like constipation and feel sluggish. Your body needs to burn off the remaining glucose and adjust to ketosis and fat for energy. This takes time. You may also feel the effects of a drop in blood sugar. It is possible if you follow this lifestyle for a long time; that you could develop kidney stones, have severe weight loss, or degeneration in your muscles. To combat these potential negative side effects, you need to balance your diet and be careful what you eat. This means choosing ingredients and foods that support your body for the long term, like chokings Keto bread made from healthy and wholesome ingredients.

Specific Achievements

The above health benefits are things you can expect to achieve with Keto bread and the Keto diet. Now here are some ideas about recipes you can create with Keto bread recipes. Of course, there is a standard bread loaf recipe, similar to a loaf of wheat bread, but there is so much more! Adapting ingredients with each to make it the best for you is also ideal, changing our ingredients as necessary for your health and taste preferences. It is also good to keep in mind that some people advise against creating these substitute meals. The reason is that they could prevent you from kicking the craving for things like bread and pizza, making it harder to resist the traditional versions. There is little evidence to support this claim, other than personal experience, and that differs from person to person. Eating these substitutes can help you forgo the feeling of hunger, cravings, and diet "restrictions." When you feel like you cannot eat something, you can get preoccupied with wanting the restricted food. Instead, you can make a healthy, Keto "approved" version and not suffer those restrictions. They are especially helpful during the early stages of the Keto diet because you can overcome temptations with these recipes.

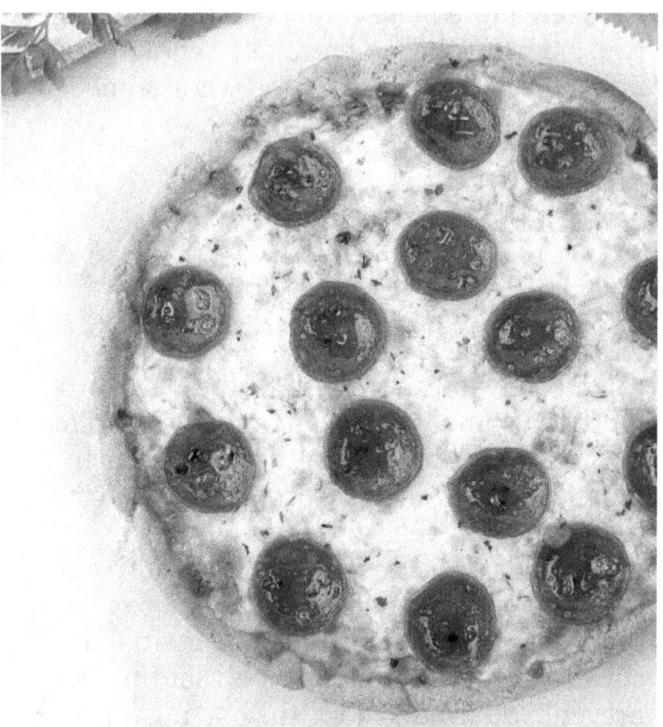

- ***Cauliflower Pizza Crust*** – No need to give up pizza! And no it is even easier by buying bags of already-riced cauliflower for your crispy crust.
- ***Waffles*** – Another morning treat is waffles, or go southern with chicken and waffles.
- ***Bagels*** – No need to give up your morning bagel with your coffee! Add

various toppings to these and enjoy adapting to recipes like bagel pizzas or bagel hot dogs.

- **_Cinnamon Rolls_** – The trick to the sweetness is monk fruit erythritol. Be careful about introducing any sweets into your diet, even healthier alternatives, because of your body's cravings. Try to eat these only for special occasions.

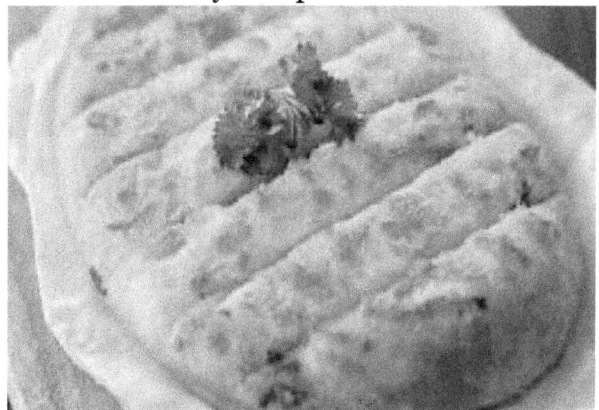

- **_Garlic, Cheesy Rolls_** – Another bread alternative great for a side dish or snack, but be aware of the carbs in these little "muffins."
- **_Soft Pretzels_** – These are not the easiest to make, but they are tasty. Use the xanthum gum to help bind the ingredients together and mimic gluten flour. Eat these sparingly because of the carb count.

- ***Tortillas*** – No need to give up tacos! Change out the seasoning in the recipe to get the flavor you prefer.

- **Cloud Bread** – Some love this bread, others hate it. Regardless, it is one of the most common or associated bread for the Keto diet. It has no carbs and can be a great substitute for sandwich bread. It can taste of eggs, so be prepared for the additional flavor.
- **Fry Bread** – Start with the standard ingredients; almond flour, coconut oil, and eggs, and then mix in cheese before cooking in oil.

- ***Coconut Zucchini Bread*** – the main ingredient in this bread is coconut flour; however, you can use almond flour if you prefer the taste and texture of almond flour instead. Just make sure you use the correct proportions for the substitution.

- ***Flatbread*** – an easy recipe with a few ingredients and only one carb. There are many flavors and topping options you can experiment with while still keeping it Keto.

- ***Pizza Pull-Apart Bread*** – eat minimally because of the carb count, but a delicious recipe for a weeknight meal or side dish.

Chapter 4: How to Start the Ketogenic Diet with Ketogenic Bread

One of the easiest ways to start following the Keto diet is by incorporating Keto bread in it at the very beginning. This makes the transition much easier and less restrictive. Your body will not be in shock, cutting out foods that it normally relied upon for energy. Instead, you are almost "tricking" your brain into thinking it is gathering energy from these sources, allowing your taste buds to enjoy the "normal" flavors and textures, but filling your body with healthy fats and little carbs. Throughout this chapter, you will learn more tips and techniques on how to being the Keto diet and how Keto bread can play a large role in your ultimate success.

Starting the Keto Diet

A lot of people consider the Keto diet more of a lifestyle choice or a way of eating. They often do not view this approach to food and health as a traditional diet. This is because it works far beyond the level of your physical weight, and dives into your health on a cellular level. It removes the sugar crashes and blood sugar spikes and drops. It helps remove cravings and stabilizes your weight. To get your body into ketosis, you need to drop your carb intake to under 20 net grams of carbs each day. This means taking the number of carbs you consume and subtracting the amount of fiber and sugar alcohol you ingest. This gives you your net carb intake. Erythritol is an example of sugar alcohol. Some sugars are counted, but some are not. This is because some are absorbed into the body and others are not. Sugar alcohols are examples of those that do not count towards your glycemic count.

If you do not want to get caught into the net carb "trap," you can choose to count your total carbs instead. This does make it harder to eat things like green vegetables and fiber-rich vegetables that also have a lot of carbs. This is best to do if you try the net carb approach but have no luck with the results after a few weeks. In addition, before moving to the "total carb" approach, cut back on the sugar alcohols and treats, even if they are low carb. Those could be the things holding your body back from its potential.

When you begin your diet with Keto bread, you can expect to help your body lose weight quickly, help stabilize your mood and energy, control your blood sugar, cut back on strong cravings, minimize your appetite, increase "good" cholesterol, decrease elevated blood pressure, improve the appearance of your skin, extend your longevity, and support your digestive tract.

Beginning your diet with Keto bread as a staple is a wise decision because it fits nicely into a Western diet as well as keeping your carbs low. It is a key food for reaching ketosis in a healthy and easy way. In addition, well-made Keto bread offers a good ratio of macronutrients, or carbs, protein, and fat. Typically, on the Keto diet, you want your meal to be made mostly of healthy fats with a little bit of protein. In addition, you want hardly any carbs present. Keto bread fits this perfectly because of the ingredients and ratios.

When your body reaches ketosis, which is a metabolic state, you are burning fat for fuel, not carbs. You are feeding your body and brain a "clean" energy source that it thrives on. This is why people talk about having a better mental focus and a healthier body when following the Keto diet. You need to restrict your carbs drastically for at least three and up to five days in order to reach this state. Those few days can be very challenging, especially the first time. You can experience symptoms similar to withdrawal. This is because your body is weaning itself off of glucose and carbs and learning how to fun on fat. This is essentially detoxing your body of the ingredient, and it is a form of withdrawal. One of the side effects you do not need to suffer is that of feeling constrained. You do not need to feel like you have given up a "normal" diet or your favorite foods, like bread. Instead, during these first few days especially, reach for healthy, Keto-approved alternatives to keep you motivated. It will not help your clarity and energy levels right away, but it will at least curb some powerful cravings.

Starting your Keto diet can seem overwhelming. It is not always easy and there is a learning curve involved. Just remember, you have to start at the beginning. Every person who has started, stuck to, and enjoyed a Keto lifestyle started where you are right now—at the beginning. And thankfully, because so many have come before, you can learn from their trials and errors along their path. One of those trials often voiced is the challenge of giving up their favorite foods like rolls, waffles, pancakes, sandwich bread, etc. To help them get past this and ease into the lifestyle better, gather great recipes and plan ahead to set yourself up for success. You can do it, too!

Some other helpful tips for starting your Keto diet include:

1. Begin recording your macronutrients on your normal, unrestricted diet. Notice what your "typical" ranges or percentages are.
2. Start cutting down on your carbs just slightly. Work on lowering your carbs by replacing favorite foods with healthier options that offer more healthy fat and less carb load. Play around with finding something that you can enjoy without

feeling restricted. After all, at this point, you are just experimenting, not dieting.
3. Begin integrating Keto bread recipes into your diet in place of your normal bread. Begin with one or two recipes that you tweak and refine to fit into your life, palette, and budget. Work on replacing all your bread for a length of time.
4. Now start cutting down your carbs so that they are less than 20 grams of net carbs. Do not worry about fat and protein just yet, just focus on getting the carbs lower on a daily basis.
5. Once you have it worked out so that the carbs are low, move on to reduce your protein intake. Do not wait too long to cut back on your protein to help support your kidneys, but also so you start to see more results in your weight, skin, and health. Set a goal for protein and make it a game to see if you can hit it without going over or under, and also staying within your carb goals.
6. Play around with fats. This is the ingredient that you can increase and decrease, as you need to. Increase the fat in your diet by dipping your Keto bread in some herbed oils, for example. But if you are looking to lose weight, do not focus on getting in all your fats. If you feel satisfied, do not push it. Just enjoy your day!
7. Once you have worked on your foods, take a look at your drinks. Until this

point, you have not had any restrictions on what you can drink. It is time to look at it. Drinking a lot of water is great. Try to drink about 16 cups of water every day. You can have a cup or two of tea or coffee, but be careful about the additives you put into them. Also, watch out for caffeine and its sneaky ways.

8. Increase your electrolytes. Sometimes you can feel tired because your body needs to replace the magnesium and potassium that is flushed out of your body by all that water. To balance this out, drink bone broth or add a healthy dose of salt to your meals. Pickled vegetables like sauerkraut and kimchi are also good sources. Try to find ways to incorporate these into your diet on a daily basis. Adding sea salt to a flatbread recipe is an excellent method for sticking to your Keto bread and increasing electrolytes.

9. Add in exercise at the end. It is unnecessary with this diet plan, but it can help move it along faster and make you feel better.

Chapter 5: Anti-aging, Weight Loss, and More

Keto bread is a key food in your Keto diet and the benefits you can enjoy. Things, like losing weight, reducing the effects of aging, and lowering chronic inflammation, can be achieved with your Keto bread.

Weight Loss

As explained earlier in this book, when you follow the Keto diet you drop into a state of ketosis, a metabolic state where you change from burning carbs as glucose for fuel, and switch to burning fat instead. When you change out your "traditional" bread for Keto bread, you allow your body to enjoy the taste but none of the side effects. In fact, you get to enjoy the benefits of the Keto diet as well as the taste of bread. When you eat Keto bread, your liver is activated to turn the fat from the bread into ketone molecules. This is then used for fuel in place of the gluten it would have used with normal bread. The more ketones you produce and the less glucose you consume, your body dips into ketosis. This is the best metabolic state you can be in to lose weight.

When you are in ketosis and following the Keto diet, you will find yourself less hungry. This is because the ketones created from the Keto bread or other Keto-approved foods control the hormone released for hunger, ghrelin. In addition to suppressing this hormone, it increases the satiety hormone, cholecystokinin. This means you will be less inclined to over eat or snack between meals, simply because your hormones are controlled. You may find yourself going long periods without eating simply because you are not feeling hungry like you used to.

In addition to impacting your glucose, or blood sugar, your body influences the level of insulin in your body. The more fat you take into your body, the lower the levels of insulin. Insulin is what signals your body to store up energy. It interprets what is eaten and tells the body to store the energy as either glucose or fat. If you have a lot of insulin, you will have a lot of fat storage. Lower the amount of insulin in the body, and the more fat gets used as energy. Leptin is the signal that is sent to your brain when you are full. If you have too much insulin in your body the leptin is blocked on its path. This leads to overeating and not feeling satisfied after a meal. If you lower your insulin levels with low carbs and higher fat, you give a "fast track" for the leptin to reach your brain. This allows you to feel full and satisfied faster and longer.

Finally, when you eat fat you feel fuller for a longer period of time. You are more satisfied after a meal and more satisfied hours later. In addition, you do not experience the highs and lows of glucose-induced energy. This is because your blood sugar remains at a stable and healthy level, unlike when you eat a significant amount of carbs. In order for your body to keep going when it is running on glucose, it needs a steady intake of carbs to convert into that energy. This is why you feel hungry again after only a few hours of eating. But if you eat a high-fat, low-carb meal, and you are fueling your body with fat instead, you will feel full for a longer period of time. You will experience fewer cravings and more stable hormones as well. All of this leads to weight loss, and additional health benefits, like reducing the effects of age.

Anti-aging

The effects of aging happen to every person, but some more rapidly than others. At Gladstone Institute, some researchers think they may have found an answer as well as a metaphorical "fountain of youth." The Keto diet suggests that it has the ability to delay and even reverse the effects of aging on the human body. The current healthcare system in America is consumed with the aging population suffering from the effects of aging, like heart disease. But the research published from Gladstone Institute in the journal, *Science*, the researchers suggest that these diseases can be significantly reduced. Even Alzheimer's and cancer have been shown to be positively impacted by those following the Keto diet.

Time and time again studies on animals and adults have shown that restricting calories helps slow the aging process. It can be in part because it helps reduce the risk of developing a variety of disease but also because it simply supports the health of your body. The director of the Center for HIV and Aging at Gladstone Institute, and the senior author of the research published in the journal, Science, Dr. Verdin does explain that while the research is clear, the reason is not. It could be linked to the B-hydroxybutyrate. This is a chemical compound that is released when a body begins to starve. This is a critical compound for the aging process. When you are eating Keto bread and on the Keto diet you can bring on the production of this chemical. This could be the key, but more research is necessary.

It is possible as the "magical" compound because it is produced in periods where the body is concerned about its energy source, like while exercising or fasting, and it is shown to block oxidative stress. Oxidative stress is what causes cells to age, and therefore your body to age. However, if these compounds, or even ketones, get too high in the body it can be a bad thing. For type-one diabetics, for example, it can be extremely dangerous. But in most people, low levels of ketones are good and beneficial. While the research is still new and limited, the effects are promising. Another reason it is possible to support your health and longevity is because it reduces chronic inflammation in your body.

Chronic Inflammation Management

Inflammation is a natural and intuitive body response to invaders. Invaders in your body can be an infection, disease, or things like a broken bone or dust in your eye. But when this inflammation continues, it turns from helping your body and turns to hurt it. It is this inflammation that you want to reduce. Chronic inflammation is linked to a series of serious diseases. It is unclear if it causes these diseases or a result, but it exists in just about all cases of health problems like cancer, cognitive disorders, cardiac issues, and more. The best way to control inflammation in your body is through lifestyle choices, like your diet. Changing into a state of ketosis inhibits inflammation in some situations, especially if it is not necessary like to fight an infection or disease. In addition to blocking inflammation pathways, a Keto diet opens a regulatory pathway, AMPK. It is a powerful tool for calming chronic inflammation.

Conclusion

Thank you again for downloading this book, *Ketogenic Bread*!

Hopefully, throughout this book, you found helpful information and ideas for how to integrate and embrace Keto bread in your diet. It can be hard making choices about your health with all the information out there. Some can be more confusing than others. It is important that you do your research and learns more about what you plan to do for your health. This book was designed to help you understand more about the choice to include Keto bread into your diet and why it is beneficial.

The design of this book is to introduce you to one food that is versatile, healthy, and beneficial for your Keto lifestyle choice. Keto bread can come in a variety of different forms and serve in several different ways. Some of the main ingredients used in the bread recipes are outlined to help you see their individual health benefits, as well as exploring the general health benefits of the Keto diet. Finally, hopefully, you discovered why including Keto bread in your diet is beneficial. There are so many ways and reasons you should start and include Keto bread in your Keto lifestyle. And there are so many delicious recipes you can try out!

www.ingramcontent.com/pod-product-compliance
Lightning Source LLC
Chambersburg PA
CBHW071324080526
44587CB00018B/3345